AMAZING HUMAN FEATS OF Survival

by Annette Gulati

Raintree is an imprint of Capstone Global Library Limited, a company incorporated in England and Wales having its registered office at 264 Banbury Road, Oxford, OX2 7DY – Registered company number: 6695582

www.raintree.co.uk
myorders@raintree.co.uk

Edited by Meg Gaertner
Designed by Becky Daum
Production by Craig Hinton
Originated by Capstone Global Library Ltd
Printed and bound in India

ISBN 978 1 4747 7518 2
22 21 20 19 18
10 9 8 7 6 5 4 3 2 1

ISBN 978 1 4747 7342 3
23 22 21 20 19
10 9 8 7 6 5 4 3 2 1

British Library Cataloguing in Publication Data
A full catalogue record for this book is available from the British Library.

Acknowledgements
We would like to thank the following for permission to reproduce photographs: AP Images: E. Pablo Kosmicki, 14; iStockphoto: amygdala_imagery, 13, DieterMeyrl, cover, ganglium, 11, ToniFlap, 23, 28, Zysman, 10–11; Shutterstock, Adwo, 26–27, Amelie Koch, 25, iremt, 21, kastianz, 17, Makasana Photo ... Salparadis, 8–9. Design Elements: iStockpho ...

Every effort has bee ... ed in this book. Any omissions will be re ... blisher.

All the internet add ... oing to press. However, due to th ... e changed, or sites may have changed ... publisher regret any inconvenience this ... can be accepted by either the author o ...

CONTENTS

SURVIVAL

A young woman survived a plane crash. A man's arm was crushed by a 360-kilogram (800-pound) rock. Two men were trapped on a mountain. A family was lost at sea.

These people faced difficult situations. But they stayed positive. They did not give up hope. They used skills to help them survive.

Survival situations, such as a plane crash, often happen unexpectedly.

NOSEDIVE

Juliane Koepcke and her mother were flying home for Christmas in 1971. Koepcke was 17 years old. The aeroplane flew into a dark cloud. Lightning struck the engine of the plane. Koepcke was scared when the plane began to **nosedive**. She fainted.

The average passenger plane is struck by lightning approximately once per year.

The jungle has a
thick canopy.

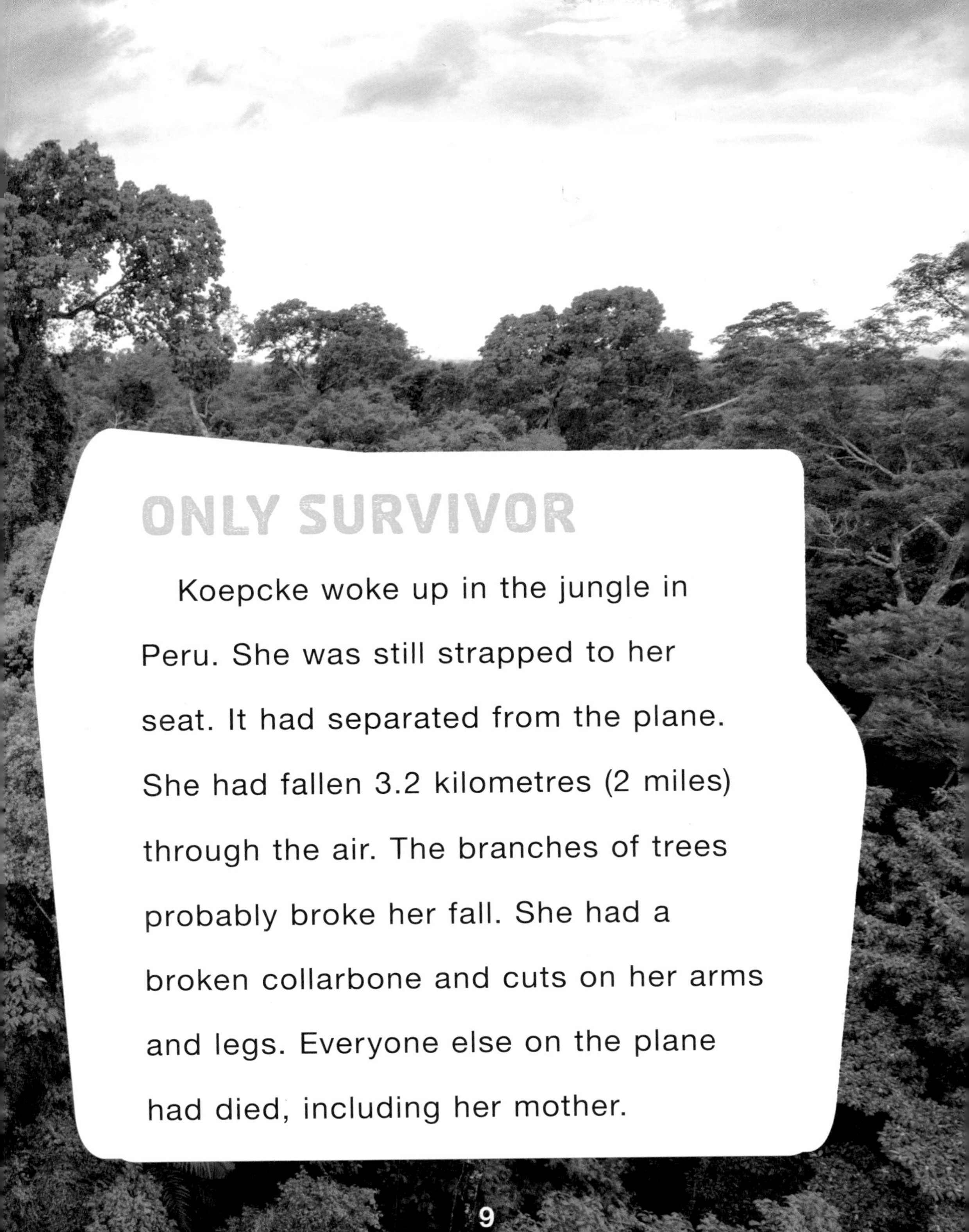

ONLY SURVIVOR

Koepcke woke up in the jungle in Peru. She was still strapped to her seat. It had separated from the plane. She had fallen 3.2 kilometres (2 miles) through the air. The branches of trees probably broke her fall. She had a broken collarbone and cuts on her arms and legs. Everyone else on the plane had died, including her mother.

More than 90 different types of snakes live in Peru.

ALL ALONE

Koepcke had only one bag of sweets to eat. She walked through streams and looked for help. Crocodiles and snakes hid nearby. **Maggots** filled her **wounds**. She was alone for 10 days. Finally, some forest workers helped her to safety.

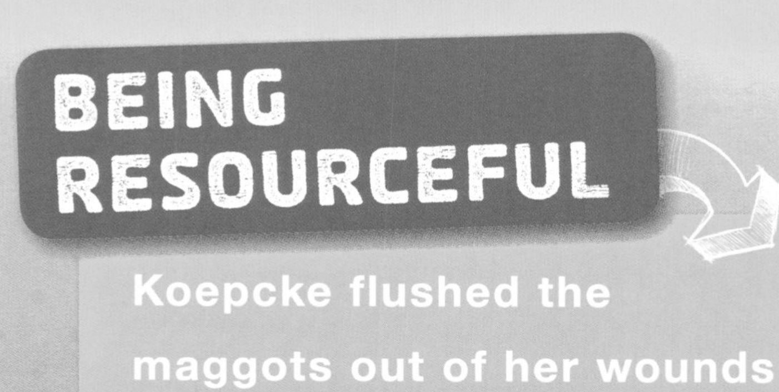

Koepcke flushed the maggots out of her wounds with petrol.

White caimans are part of the crocodile family. They hide in water to catch their prey.

CHAPTER 3

HIKING Alone

Aron Ralston set out alone on an eight-hour hike in 2003. He was exploring a **deserted** area of Utah, USA. Ralston had some supplies. But he did not tell anyone where he was going. He entered a narrow rock canyon.

Suddenly he slipped. A 360-kilogram (800-pound) rock fell on his arm. He tried to chip away at the rock with his knife. But it did not work. He was trapped.

Hikers should travel in groups. They should let others know where they are going.

Ralston was fitted with a fake arm after the accident.

A DIFFICULT CHOICE

Ralston soon ran out of food and water. He thought he was going to die. After six days, he made a decision. He used his knife to cut off his forearm. It was very painful. But he was free. Ralston made it to the canyon floor. He met a family who helped him.

NO WATER

Ralston drank his own urine to stay alive.

CHAPTER 4

CLIMBING AND Falling

Joe Simpson and Simon Yates were climbing in the Andes Mountains in 1985. On the way down, Simpson broke his leg. Yates tried to help him. He used a rope to connect Simpson to himself. He carefully lowered Simpson down a ledge on the rope. Then he made his way down to his friend. Yates repeated these two actions many times.

The Andes Mountains cross seven countries in South America.

Mountain climbers take ropes and other life-saving equipment with them.

CUTTING THE ROPE

Then a blizzard began. Simpson fell off a ledge. Yates thought he was dead. He was afraid he would die too. He decided to cut the rope. Simpson fell further. Yates made it back to camp. But he felt sad and guilty. Four days later, Simpson came back to camp. He was **frostbitten** and starving. He had pulled himself out of an ice cave. Then he had crawled 10 kilometres (6 miles) back to camp.

SHIPWRECK

Dougal and Lyn Robertson went on a family trip in the 1970s. They and their four children left England on their boat, *Lucette*. The family sailed for 17 months. One day, three killer whales hit the boat. The boat began to sink. The family squeezed onto a small lifeboat. They ate turtles and fish to survive. A fishing boat rescued them 38 days later.

Lucette was a wooden schooner similar to this one.

CHAPTER 6

THE JUNGLE

Yossi Ghinsberg nearly died in the Amazon rainforest in 1981. He was backpacking with friends in Bolivia. The group split up. Some of the men wanted to walk. But Ghinsberg chose to raft along the river. The raft went over a waterfall.

Ghinsberg survived the fall, but he was lost. He fought off snakes and spiders. He survived a jaguar attack. He set fire to his insect spray to make a flamethrower. He ate fruit and raw eggs from birds' nests. His friends found him three weeks later. Ghinsberg could barely walk.

Approximately 3,600 species of spiders live in the Amazon jungle.

CHAPTER 7

POLAR Expedition

Ernest Shackleton set out for the South Pole with 28 men in 1915. Their ship, the *Endurance*, got trapped in ice. The men camped on the ice for more than one year. Finally, the ice melted. The men escaped in lifeboats.

Shackleton went on three separate trips to icy Antarctica.

Shackleton took a similar lifeboat from Elephant Island to South Georgia across 1,500 kilometres (920 miles) of ocean.

COLD AND STRANDED

The men sailed for Elephant Island off the coast of Antarctica. When they reached the island, it was deserted. Shackleton knew nobody would find them. He sailed to another island with five men. They walked 51 kilometres (32 miles) to find help. They had been lost for two years. All the men survived.

GLOSSARY

deserted
area that is empty of people

frostbitten
injured by frost

maggot
young form of a fly

nosedive
fall suddenly

wound
injury on the body

OTHER AMAZING FEATS

- Roy Sullivan is a US park ranger. He has survived being struck by lightning seven times.
- Ada Blackjack was an Inuit woman. She spent two years alone in the Arctic. She taught herself how to hunt in order to survive.
- Petra Nemcova is a model. She clung to a palm tree for eight hours during the 2004 tsunami in Thailand.

ACTIVITY

SURVIVAL KIT

Natural disasters occur all over the world. Research a natural disaster that might happen where you live. How could you be prepared for that natural disaster? Search online for tools and items that would help you survive such a disaster. Make a list of items. Help your family collect the items for a survival kit.

FIND OUT MORE

Amazed by these feats of survival and curious to learn more? Check out these resources:

Books

Adrift and Alone: True Stories of Survival at Sea, Nel Yomtov (Raintree, 2015)

Bear Grylls Survival Skills Handbook: Dangers and Emergencies, Bear Grylls (Bear Grylls, 2017)

Jungle Survival Handbook, Jen Green (Miles Kelly, 2014)

Survivng the Wilderness (Extreme Survival), Michael Hurley (Raintree, 2012)

Websites

Learn about another famous polar explorer.
www.bbc.co.uk/newsround/16084213

Find out more about the amazon rainforest.
www.dkfindout.com/uk/animals-and-nature/habitats-and-ecosystems/amazon-rainforest

INDEX